crafting
with kids

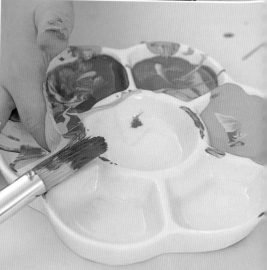

photography by
vanessa davies

catherine woram

crafting
with kids

creative fun for
children aged 3–10

RYLAND
PETERS
& SMALL
LONDON NEW YORK

First published in the United
States in 2006 by
Ryland Peters & Small, Inc
519 Broadway, Fifth Floor
New York, NY 10012
www.rylandpeters.com

10 9 8 7 6 5

Text, design, and photographs
© Ryland Peters & Small 2006

ISBN-978-1-84597-252-3

Library of Congress Cataloging-in-Publication
Data

Woram, Catherine.
  Crafting with kids : creative fun for children
aged 3-10 / Catherine Woram
; photography by Vanessa Davies.
    p. cm.
  Includes index.
  ISBN-13: 978-1-84597-252-3
  ISBN-10: 1-84597-252-X
  1. Handicraft--Juvenile literature. I. Title.

TT160.W67 2006
745.5--dc22
                              2006016003

Senior designer Catherine Griffin
Commissioning editor Annabel
Morgan
Picture research Emily Westlake
Production Gordana Simakovic
Art director Anne-Marie Bulat
Publishing director Alison Starling

Text and styling Catherine Woram

Printed and bound in China

contents

get creative and crafty...

I must confess to a lifelong passion for crafts—my mother remembers finding me on her sewing machine at the age of seven, inserting a zipper into a skirt I had just made. She didn't know whether to be cross that I had used the machine without her permission or delighted at her eldest daughter's budding sewing skills! She still has many of the items we crafted as children, and it is this aspect of crafting that makes it so appealing. There is nothing better than a handmade gift or card from a child, because it is unique.

The projects in this book cover a wide selection of different crafting techniques, from papier mâché to tie-dye. Each project is accompanied by step-by-step photographs, and there are suggestions for other items that can be made using the same basic technique. If your kids love crafting (and most do), it's a good idea to create a craft box or to devote a kitchen cupboard to craft materials. Squirrel away pieces of string and ribbon, scraps of fabric, and leftover wrapping paper. Many of the projects make use of basic household items such as newspapers and jam jars, which is a great way of recycling them. Teach your child to look after their tools, and to clean them after they have finished crafting.

One of the most rewarding aspects of the creation of the book was seeing how the children enjoyed the crafts. My daughters, Jessica (aged eight) and Anna (aged six), helped with many projects and were a constant source of inspiration. I'm sure that you'll enjoy making the projects in the book as much as your children will, and that your friends and relatives will delight in receiving them as gifts, too.

paint

Any painting undertaken in our house inevitably ends up with the children painting parts of themselves, too! So, if a project requires them to paint themselves, they are sure to enjoy it. Paint-and-bake ceramic kits that can be "fired" in a domestic oven are ideal for this project.

finger- and hand-painting

YOU WILL NEED:
plate or other object to be decorated • specialty paints for china • paintbrushes in various sizes • saucers to hold the paints

paint hands In separate saucers or on a paint tray, put out a small amount of each of the paint colors to be used. Use a thick brush to apply the paint to the palm of the hand. Make sure that the paint is not too thick. It's a good idea to keep a cloth close by in case of accidents.

practice printing Before attempting to decorate your plate, or other chosen object, help your child to practice first, to get the technique right. The hand needs to be pressed as flat as possible, with the fingers slightly splayed to show the shape. Once the printing technique has been mastered on paper, you can move on to the real thing.

print on plate Clean off any excess paint from the practice run, and reapply fresh paint to the hand. You can use one color, or you can paint different fingers in different colors. Press the hand flat with fingers splayed, as before. Carefully lift the hand off the plate and let the paint dry.

finish off Apply a coat of paint to the fingertips and print around the edge of the plate to create a border. The child may also like to write his or her name on the plate. To fix the paint, bake the item in the oven, following the manufacturer's instructions, or take it to a pottery café to be fired.

framed picture

Fingertips can be used to create all sorts of shapes or designs, including animals, flowers, and abstract patterns. This pretty bouquet of flowers in a palette of bright pinks, oranges, and reds was made using the fingertips. The simple vase was painted in using a brush. Fingertip prints were also used to decorate the painted frame.

painted plates

A palm print decorates the center of this plate, while the border is finger-painted in alternate colors of red and mauve. To celebrate the birth of a new baby, try painting the soles of the baby's feet and decorating a plate, to keep as a memory of those tiny feet.

painted tray

A simple wooden tray decorated by your child makes a delightful gift for a grandmother or godmother, or even your child's schoolteacher. The words "TEA TIME" were painted using fingertips, while the corners of the tray were decorated with two bold handprints. Finish a wooden object such as a tray with a couple of coats of water-based acrylic varnish, to seal the paint and protect the design.

little tips

You can find a wide variety of unfired ceramic objects at paint-your-own-china shops. Many stores will be happy for you to purchase an item and decorate it at home, then the store will fire it for you at a later date.

YOU WILL NEED:
medium-sized potato •
star-shaped cookie cutter •
chopping board • sharp knife
(to be used by an adult only) •
kitchen paper or dry cloth •
paints in your chosen colors •
saucers to hold the paints •
plain paper

cut your shape
Cut the potato in half, making sure the surface of the potato is as flat as possible. Place the cookie cutter on a cutting board with the sharp edge facing upwards. Press the potato down onto the cutter. An adult can now cut away the potato around the outside of the star using a knife.

dip in paint
If the potato is particularly wet, blot it on paper towels or a dry cloth. Pour out the various paint colors into different saucers. Dip the potato into the paint, making sure that the whole star shape is covered in paint.

get printing
Begin printing with the potato star on the plain paper. To ensure the design prints properly, show the child how to use a gentle rocking motion, moving the potato from side to side without lifting it from the paper. This will help to apply the paint evenly, even if the potato is not completely flat.

add more colors
If you wish to use different colors, wash or wipe the paint off the potato and allow it to dry. (It may be quicker to cut another design from the remaining half of the potato.) Continue printing in another color, then allow the design to dry.

Potato printing is a traditional technique that is a favorite with children of all ages—and it's very inexpensive, too! You can experiment with other fruit and vegetables, including apples, rhubarb, and pears. The potatoes can be cut using cookie cutters, or an adult could use a sharp knife to cut out a few different shapes by hand.

potato printing

wrap it up

We used a simple star shape and printed
with red paint onto plain white paper to
create this festive Christmas gift wrap.
The large-sized ledger photocopier paper
is perfect for this project.

dish towels

Fruit and vegetable printing works equally well on fabric. We used an apple print in red and green on plain white cotton for these fun dish towels, which would make a very practical yet pretty gift.

print pictures

Cut large apples in half to print these fun pictures in bold red and fresh green tones. We carefully added the stalk detail using a fine paintbrush. The prints were placed in frames painted in contrasting colors before hanging them on the wall.

little tips

If you are potato-printing on fabric, make sure that you use fabric or stencil paint, so the item can be washed • Take note of the manufacturer's instructions on how to make the paint "fix"—some paint needs be fixed with a hot iron.

This is a perfect project for toddlers,
who will be fascinated by the process.
You may have to do the painting in stages—
for example, the lion's face first, then the
mane—otherwise the paint dries too quickly.

mirror-image painting

YOU WILL NEED:
plain paper • pencil • paints
in your chosen colors •
paintbrushes in various sizes •
saucers to hold the paints •
small pompom for lion's nose,
if required

fold paper in half Fold the paper in half, pressing down flat to form a crease. Open up the paper and draw a semicircle on one side of the paper in pencil (you may like to use a plate to draw a more accurate circle).

start painting Fill in the semicircle with paint. It is important to do this fairly quickly, or the paint will start to dry and will not transfer properly to the other side of the paper when it is folded.

fold over Fold the paper in half on the original crease and press down firmly. Open the paper to reveal the mirror image of the face. The next stage is the lion's mane—again, it may be easier to draw this before painting. Fill in the triangles with paint, fold the paper in half, and open up to reveal the mane.

finish off Fill in one eye and half of the mouth using brown paint. Fold the paper in half, press it flat, and open to reveal the face of the lion. As a finishing touch, we added a small pompom for the lion's nose.

YOU WILL NEED:
paints in your chosen colors •
paintbrushes in various sizes •
saucers to hold the paints • one
large stone for the body • two
small round stones for the eyes •
two flat oval-shaped stones for
the feet • strong glue

paint stones
Paint the large stone for the body green all over and let it dry. For the best results, apply a second coat and let dry. We painted the top of the stone first, and waited until it was completely dry before painting the underside. Paint the smaller stones green and let them dry.

add the details
Paint the spots on using a darker shade of green paint. If you want very regular spots, draw them on the stone first, using a pencil. Fill in the spots using a finer paintbrush. Now use a fine paintbrush and white paint to paint on the frog's mouth.

paint eyes and feet
Paint the small round stones for the eyes with a circle of white paint for the frog's eyes, then let dry. Now, using a finer paintbrush, paint on the black eyeballs. Decorate the flatter oval stones for the frog's feet with dark green spots to match the body.

finish off
Use strong glue to fix the frog's eyes to the top of the body. Repeat for the feet on the underside of the stone. Let dry completely.

Painted stones can be used to create a variety of items, such as paperweights, jewelry, and bookends. The shape of the stone may inspire its design—ask your child what the stone looks like, and what they think it could be made into.

painted stones

friendship stones

These pretty friendship stones have been decorated with simple flower motifs, allowing the natural colors of the stone to show through. Use a pencil to write your friend's name or a message on the underside of the stone.

frog bookend

One large stone and four smaller stones were used to create this handsome frog bookend (see pages 20–21 for the full technique). You could make a pair of them to sit on a bookshelf to support your books.

ladybug paperweight

To create these cute little paperweights, use bright red paint to cover stones of various different sizes. Use a finer paintbrush to add the ladybug markings in black, then dab on tiny white dots to depict the eyes.

little tips

It is important to remember that is illegal to remove stones from beaches in certain countries • Garden centers sell bags of stones in assorted sizes • You may like to finish stones with a couple of coats of water-based acrylic varnish to seal the paint when the projects are finished. Let the varnish dry completely between coats.

Stenciling can be used to decorate many items—paper, card stock, wood, and fabric. You can buy cardboard or plastic stencils, both of which are easy to use. Single stencils are better for younger children, who may be confused by repeat patterns, as they are quite tricky to position correctly.

stenciling

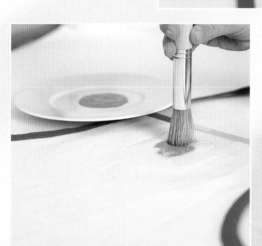

position the stencil

Place the stencil onto the apron in the position to be stenciled. Use pieces of masking tape on each corner to hold the stencil securely in place. It is important that the stencil is not moved during the stenciling process, as this will cause the design to smudge.

apply the paint

Dip the stenciling brush into the paint and remove as much excess paint as possible by wiping it on a cloth or paper towels. If there is too much paint on the brush, it will leak through the edges of the stencil and the outline may "bleed." Let the paint dry slightly before removing the stencil.

remove the stencil

When the paint is dry (or almost dry), peel off the masking tape and lift the stencil to reveal the design. Repeat patterns usually have markings at the corners to help you get the spacing right, so make sure you have marked these before taking off the stencil.

repeat the pattern

Place the stencil in the correct position and repeat the design, first removing any excess paint on a cloth or paper towel. When you have finished and the apron is dry, fix the fabric paint with a hot iron, as per the manufacturer's instructions.

aprons or dish towels

These simple aprons are made in natural unbleached cotton edged in red and pink bias binding. We used a simple heart-shaped stencil to decorate the edges of the red apron, while the pink apron features a fun cookie stencil, which is a two-part design stenciled in beige with pink icing. See pages 24–25 for the full technique.

decorated box

Boys will love keeping their special treasures in this hand-painted wooden box. We applied two coats of pale blue paint to the box, letting it dry thoroughly between coats. Next, we decorated the box using a traditional toy-soldier stencil in bold dark blue paint, which really stands out on the light blue background. The soldier design is also repeated on the lid of the box. To finish, we applied a couple of coats of water-based acrylic varnish, which seals the paint and protects the design.

little tips

Young children are not renowned for their patience, and waiting for paint to dry is difficult. Have a hairdryer handy, so that the paint can be quickly dried on a warm setting (but keep it out of the reach of children, as hairdryers are a fire hazard) • If you are making a gift, always practice the technique first on paper.

fabric

Weaving is fun for most ages except the very young. The technique is easy to accomplish and can be applied to both two- and three-dimensional projects. Children will love making cushions and bags from woven ribbons, as well as pen cups or boxes using colored pipe cleaners.

weaving

YOU WILL NEED:
four spools of different-colored ribbon, each one about ¾-inch (2-cm) wide • pins • square of fabric about 18 x 18 inches (45 x 45 cm) • needle and thread • scissors

cut the ribbon Cut the ribbon into 18-inch (45-cm) lengths and divide into separate piles by color for easier selection when weaving. We used brightly colored satin ribbons, although you could substitute pretty pastels or even strips of fabric cut with pinking shears.

pin along edge Carefully arrange the pieces of ribbon down one side of the fabric square, alternating two different colors. Pin the ribbons in place using one pin per piece of ribbon to hold them secure during the weaving. Next, pin the remaining ribbons, in alternating colors, along the other edge, so that they're ready for weaving.

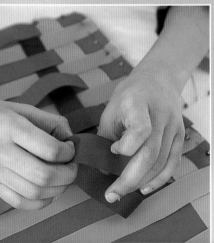

start weaving Start with the ribbon nearest to the row of pins. Thread the ribbon over the first piece of ribbon and under the next and repeat until you reach the other side of the fabric square. Pin the ribbon in place. Repeat with the other ribbon color until the weaving is finished. Pin each piece of ribbon in place to stop it from slipping.

stitch to base Use a needle and thread to tack neatly around the four sides of the weaving, stitching the ribbons to the fabric square.

pen and pencil holder

Use the same weaving technique as shown on pages 30–31 but using colored pipe cleaners. Fold the finished product around an empty can or jar to create this fun pencil holder. The ends of the pipe cleaners are folded over inside the can and folded flat at the bottom. To finish, twist the ends of the pipe cleaners together and trim the edges with scissors.

bag

This fun bag is made using the same technique as shown on pages 30–31, but using satin and velvet ribbons in different widths. The bag is backed in plain cotton and the strap is made using two lengths of ribbon in different colors. To finish, we added a cute little butterfly made from twisted pipe-cleaners.

cushion

To make the woven ribbon into a cushion cover, cut another fabric square measuring 18 x 18 inches (45 x 45 cm). With the right sides facing, stitch the two pieces together on three sides. Turn right side out, insert a cushion pad, and hand-stitch to close the open end. Alternatively, press the ribbon edges under and stitch the weaving onto a ready-made cushion cover. A wool flower corsage adds the finishing touch.

little tips

With younger children, try weaving strips of colored paper and glue the edges in place • Fabric scraps can be substituted for ribbons, but it is important to trim the edges with pinking shears to prevent them from fraying.

Even younger children will enjoy making these animal finger puppets from felt. Very young children can glue rather than stitch them, as this eliminates the problem of sharp needles. Look through picture books for other ideas, and ask your child to draw any other animals he or she would like to make.

finger puppets

YOU WILL NEED:
paper for templates • pencil •
scissors • pins • squares of felt
in assorted colors • pinking
shears • needle and thread •
glue • three-dimensional
fabric paint

pin and cut out Trace the
templates on page 119 onto paper
and cut them out. Pin the templates
to the felt. Carefully cut out the felt.
You will need two body shapes per
puppet. We used pinking shears to cut
out the bodies, but normal scissors
will do, as felt does not fray.

sew body pieces together Holding two
body pieces together, hand-stitch around the edges using a
running stitch in matching thread. Leave the bottom section
open. If younger children are unable to sew, the edges can
be glued together. When making the sheep puppet, fold a
pleat in the base of the two ear shapes (as shown on the
template) and tuck the ends of the ears inside the body
sections before stitching in place.

glue on the heads For the lion puppet, apply neat dots of glue to
the back of the mane and carefully place it on the front of the finger puppet.
Push down firmly, then let it dry completely. For the sheep puppet, glue on
the little white face section and let it dry.

finish off Use three-dimensional
fabric paint to carefully draw the nose
and eyes onto the finger puppets.
Let it dry completely.

YOU WILL NEED:

cardboard for pompom discs • pencil • scissors • assorted balls of wool

wind the wool

Trace the pompom disc template on page 118 onto paper and cut it out. Place it on a piece of cardboard and draw around it. Repeat. Cut out two discs. Start to wind wool around the two discs. When the first ball of wool is finished, tie the end of the ball to the beginning of a new one. Wind the wool around the disc until it is completely covered.

cut around the outside

When the winding process is complete, hold the pompom discs securely, then cut around the edges of the wool using scissors. The wool will come away and look like fringing at this point, and it is important that the two discs are firmly held together.

secure the wool

Cut two pieces of wool about 8 inches (20 cm) long and thread them between the two cardboard discs. Pull together tightly and tie in a knot. It is a good idea to tie several knots so that the wool is very secure.

pull apart and finish off

Gently pull away the cardboard discs from the pompom. If it proves difficult, just cut them off. Trim any excess bits of wool and fluff the pompom ball to give it a nice round shape.

pompoms

**Old-fashioned pompoms are so
easy to make and are a great way
of using up leftover wool. They can
be made in a variety of sizes and
used to create toys, including cute
kittens and fluffy chicks for Easter,
as well as fun jewelry and
decorations for bags and cushions.**

pompom kittycats

These cute little cats are made using two different-sized pompoms made from the same dark gray wool. Use the ends of the pompom ties to join the two pompoms together before trimming the ends. We added little ears snipped from a piece of gray felt, some black wool whiskers, and a little gray wool tail to finish.

cream

cushion

These fun cushions are made from colored wool fabric with felt petals stitched to one corner to form a simple flower motif. We added contrastingly colored pompoms to the center of the flowers to give the cushions an interesting three-dimensional design.

flower bag

A pompom forms the center of a bold flower that decorates a pretty handmade bag made from colored wool fabric. Use two rectangles of fabric to make the bag. Place the fabric right sides together and stitch around three sides, leaving one shorter end open. Finish the handles with neat blanket stitch. Sew five fabric petals to one side of the bag, and finish the flower by stitching a pompom to the center.

little tips

Try making pompoms using different colored wools combined together, which gives a fun multicolor effect • Remember that the more times the wool is wrapped around the disc, the fuller and bouncier the finished pompom will be.

These simple heart-shaped lavender bags make great gifts and are very easy to make. Use colored felt or scraps of cotton cut with pinking shears to prevent the fabric from fraying. Fill them with dried lavender and decorate with ribbons, buttons, and bows to finish.

lavender pockets

YOU WILL NEED:
plain paper • scissors • pins • colored felt squares or scraps of cotton fabric • pinking shears • needle • embroidery thread • loose dried lavender • button • 8 inches (20 cm) of narrow ribbon

pin in position
Trace the heart template on page 118 onto a piece of plain paper and cut it out. Lay two pieces of felt or cotton fabric on top of one another, and pin the heart template to the fabric.

cut out
Using the pinking shears, carefully cut all the way around the heart template, making sure you are cutting neatly through both layers of fabric. The pinking shears give an attractive zig-zag effect to the edge of the fabric, which also stops it from fraying and means it doesn't have to be hemmed. If you are making more than one lavender heart, it's a good idea to cut them all out at the same time.

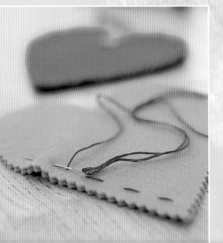

stitch
Thread the needle with the embroidery thread (use a short piece of thread, as longer pieces can get tangled, which is very frustrating). Start a simple running stitch at the bottom point of the heart and continue all the way around the heart, leaving an opening of around 1½ inches (4 cm).

fill and finish off
Fill the heart with lavender before continuing the stitching to close the heart. Using 8 inches (20 cm) of narrow ribbon, make a hanging loop and stitch it to the center of the heart. Glue on a button to cover the end of the ribbon.

YOU WILL NEED:
20-inch (50-cm) square of card stock • 24-inch (60-cm) square of blue cotton fabric • 24 x 12 inches (60 x 30 cm) green cotton fabric • other colored cotton fabrics • felt • fake fur • pompoms • popsicle sticks • glue • scissors • pinking shears • paints • fine paintbrushes

select materials Assemble the fabrics along with the paints and popsicle sticks. Glue the pale blue cotton to the card stock. Cut out the grass from the green fabric (we used pinking shears to prevent the fabric from fraying). Glue the grass section in place and let it dry.

cut out shapes Carefully cut out two tree and two cloud shapes from the felt. Cut three sheep shapes from the fur fabric, and assorted flower and fruit shapes from the colored cotton fabrics. Children may find it easier to draw the shapes on the back of the fabric with felt-tip pen before they cut them out.

place and glue shapes Once the pieces are cut out, they can be laid out on the background fabric. Your child may like to experiment with them first to see where the pieces look best. Once he or she has decided where to put each piece, they can be glued in place. Allow the glue to dry.

add details Cut out stem shapes in felt, and glue in place. Cut the popsicle sticks in half to form the fence uprights and use whole popsicle sticks for the horizontal bars. Glue them in place. Glue on the pompoms for the bunny and add felt ears. Paint in the birds in the sky and the flower centers.

Collage is enjoyed by children of all ages. Use ready-cut felt pieces for small children, who will enjoy simply glueing the shapes in place. Older children will relish cutting out their own shapes and embellishing their collages with paint, sequins, and beads.

fabric collage

wallhanging

Fabric collages make ideal wallhangings. Here, a lively country scene (see pages 42–43 for the full technique) makes a pretty wallhanging for a child's bedroom. A farmyard scene or a row of cottages would work equally well. Hang the collage from a piece of ribbon glued or stapled to the back of the collage.

tea cozy

You can use Wonder Under® or another fusible web to create fabric collages that can be machine-washed. This decorative floral tea cozy features a teacup and saucer design that has been applied to the fabric using iron-on fusible web and finished with blanket stitch and a cute spotted ribbon bow.

t-shirt

To decorate this T-shirt with a cupcake motif, we used cotton fabric backed in Wonder Under® or another fusible web. Draw a cupcake motif onto paper, then cut out a template. Pin this to your chosen fabrics, cut out the cupcake shape, and attach to the front of the T-shirt using fusible web and following the manufacturer's instructions. We added tiny red beads as a finishing touch.

little tips

Create a collage box and save pieces of ribbon, popsicle sticks, pieces of foil, cardboard, and anything you think might come in useful for creating collages · This collage method works equally well with just paper and cardboard, which is much easier for younger children to cut out and glue.

tie-dye

Tie-dyeing is a simple process with striking results. You can give old white T-shirts a new lease of life with this technique, but it is is advisable to have an adult on hand during the actual dyeing process, as it can get quite messy. Alternatively, you can follow the steps shown here to create the design, but use machine dye rather than the bucket method, as it's an easier (and less messy) option.

YOU WILL NEED:
t-shirt • string • dye in the
color of your choice • scissors •
bucket • jug • wooden spoon

tie up material Tie the string around the sleeves of the T-shirt in two places and secure tightly to ensure no dye can get through. Repeat on the body of the T-shirt, tying two pieces of string at 4-inch (10-cm) intervals. If you want additional stripes, tie more pieces of string around the T-shirt.

place item in dye Following the manufacturer's instructions, make up the dye in a bucket or large pot, adding dye fix if necessary. Push the T-shirt into the bucket of dye and stir gently with a wooden spoon to ensure the fabric is evenly covered with the dye. Leave the T-shirt for approximately one hour, stirring occasionally.

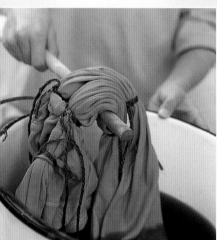

remove the t-shirt When the dye process is complete, carefully remove the T-shirt from the bucket and wash the items according to the dye manufacturer's instructions. Leave the strings in place on the T-shirt.

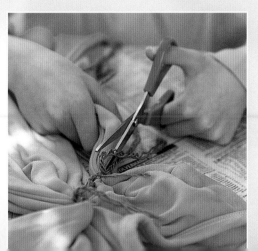

cut the strings Allow the T-shirt to dry completely. Use a pair of scissors to carefully cut the strings, taking care not to damage the T-shirt. Iron the T-shirt to remove the crease marks left by the string.

paper flowers

Paper flowers are quick and easy to make and are a great way of using up old wrapping paper and tissue. Use pipe-cleaners or drinking straws to make stems, then stand the flowers in vases made from plastic cups covered in tissue paper. Alternatively, use the flowers to make pretty jewelry or to decorate handmade cards.

YOU WILL NEED:

paper for flower template • pencil • scissors • colored card stock for the main flower shape and the flower centers • colored tissue paper or crêpe paper • stick of glue • pipe cleaners for the flower stems • Scotch tape

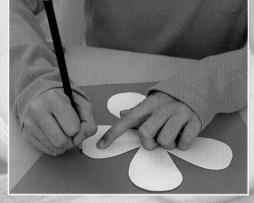

draw out flower Trace the flower template on page 118 onto paper and cut out with scissors. Draw around the template on colored card stock and cut out the flower shape carefully.

cut out petals Trace the petal template shown on page 118 and use it to cut five petals from crêpe paper or tissue paper. You can layer the flowers by cutting out five additional petals, which can be glued on top of the first petals to create a fuller effect.

glue on petals Fold a small pleat in the bottom end of each petal. Apply glue to the back of a petal and stick it to the center of the card stock flower. Repeat for each petal, allowing the glue to dry completely.

finish off Cut out a small circle of card stock, about ½ inch (1.5 cm) in diameter, and glue it to the center of the flower to cover the ends of the petals. Use a small piece of Scotch tape to attach a pipe cleaner to the back of the flower to form a stem.

hair decoration

This pretty paper flower was cut from card stock and adorned with crêpe-paper petals using the technique shown on pages 50–51. The finished flower was then glued to a sturdy hairclip.

greeting card

Glue two crêpe-paper flowers to a plain card to create a decorative three-dimensional greeting card that's perfect for birthdays or Mother's Day.

brooch

This brooch was made from card stock and crêpe paper. Cut a circle of card stock about 1¼ inches (3 cm) in diameter. Cut out six large crêpe-paper petals and six smaller crêpe-paper petals in two different colors. Glue a circle of large petals to the cardboard, and then a circle of small petals. Finish off with a pompom.

little tips

If you are using tissue paper or crêpe paper to make the flower petals, be sure to use stick glue rather than white glue, as the latter will make the paper dissolve.

Create fans using brightly colored and decorative paper—sheets of wrapping paper are a perfect choice. Finished off with long silk tassels, paper fans are quick and easy to make, and are a great addition to the dressing-up box.

fan making

YOU WILL NEED:
colored paper or wrapping
paper • scissors • glue • glitter
• silk tassels • stapler

cut out To make a paper fan, cut a piece of paper measuring about 10 x 20 inches (25 x 50 cm).

fold paper Place the sheet of paper flat on the table with the shortest edge in front of you. Starting at the end closest to you, make even folds that are about ¾ inch (2 cm) wide, turning the paper over each time to create a pleated effect. Press each fold flat (you could use a ruler to rub over the fold to make it as flat as possible).

decorate To decorate the fan, open out the pleats slightly and use glue to create a swirling pattern along the top edge of the paper. Scatter glitter over the glue and shake to remove the excess. Let the glue dry thoroughly before folding up the fan again.

finish off Pinch the pleats at the bottom of the fan firmly together, and insert the top of the silk tassel in between the central pleats. Use a stapler to secure the pleats (two or three staples are usually sufficient). If children are very young, an adult should be responsible for the stapling.

Boys and girls alike will delight in making these colorful windmills that twirl in the wind. Try making extra ones and stand them in flowerpots for fun party decorations.

paper windmills

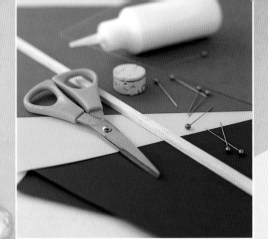

YOU WILL NEED:
two different-colored squares of paper measuring 8 x 8 inches (20 x 20 cm) • glue • scissors • card stock for the circular center • pins • small piece of cork • stick about 12 inches (30 cm) in length

choose colors Choose the colors of paper you are going to use to make the windmill. We used bold green, blue, and yellow, but soft pastels or hot pink and zingy orange look great, too.

glue and cut Apply a thin layer of glue all over the back of one sheet of paper. Carefully lay the other sheet on top and press flat. Rub firmly, making sure there are no wrinkles or air bubbles trapped between the two sheets. Allow the glue to dry completely. Now, from the corner of each square, cut a line approximately 4 inches (10 cm) long towards the center of the paper.

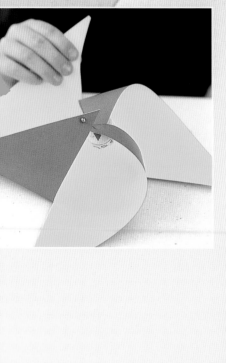

form blades With the square of paper in front of you, gently bend every other point of the paper back along the cut line and into the center. Hold in place with your fingers, and draw in the next corner. Repeat until all four corners are folded into the center.

secure with pin Push a pin through the center, making sure it goes through all four corners. It is advisable for an adult to do this. Push the pin into a cork. Using strong glue, attach the stick to the back of the cork, and let the glue dry. Glue a disc of card on to conceal the pin, if desired.

YOU WILL NEED:
paper for template • pencil •
scissors • thin card stock in
assorted colors • glue • sharp
blade to cut holes for pins (to be
used by an adult) • cotter pins
(available from most stationers)

cut out
Trace the teddy templates on page 121 onto plain paper and cut them out. Draw around the templates on a piece of card stock and cut them out. You will need twelve identical-sized ovals for the teddy's legs, arms, and ears, then one each for the nose, head, and body. We used a different-colored card stock for the teddy's nose.

glue on nose
Use glue to stick the nose to the teddy's face and let it dry completely. Lay out all the pieces of the teddy bear on a table so you can work out where the positions for the holes should be.

mark and cut holes
Use a pencil to mark the holes for the pins and make sure that each of the card sections overlaps at this point, so they will be held together by the pins. Use a sharp blade to make slits through the layers of card stock. It is advisable for an adult to do this, as blades are dangerous.

insert the cotter pins
Insert the cotter pins through each slit and fold them flat at the back of the bear. Continue until the whole teddy has been assembled. We added a decorative pin through the teddy's nose as a finishing touch.

Cotter-pin animals are fun to make and educational, too, as they teach young children about joints and movement. As you cut out and make them, describe how the sections will move when held together by the cotter pins. The pins can also be used decoratively to make buttons and eyes.

cotter-pin animals

little bunnies

Use the templates on page 120 to create these cute cotter-pin bunnies. We used card stock in two pretty shades of pink and attached the finished bunnies to a piece of ribbon with miniature wooden clothes-pegs to create a fun decoration for a child's bedroom.

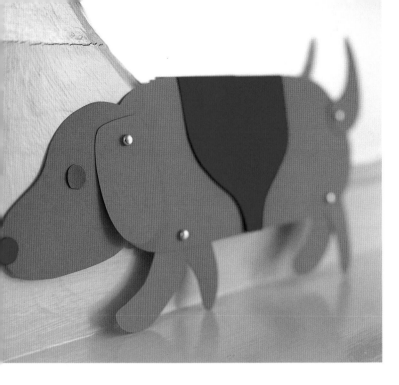

dachshund

This colorful dachshund can be made using the templates on pages 120–121 and by following the instructions on pages 58–59. The dog can be created in any length—simply elongate the body template. The dog's legs and tail are made from the same template. Add a fabric jacket for some variety.

teddy garland

Using the technique shown on pages 58–59, we made a series of cheerful teddy bears in cool greens, yellows, and blues. The teddies are strung together by their paws using cotter pins, then hung up to decorate a plain wall.

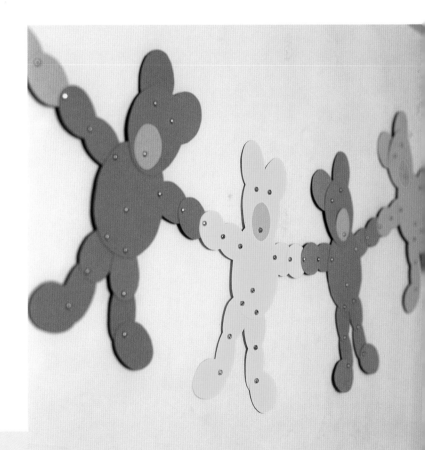

little tips

Try decorating the card stock with colorful glitter or painted decorations before joining the sections together with the cotter pins. Decorating their creations will keep the kids happily occupied for even longer!

paper chains

Traditional paper chains are so easy to make, and look fantastic at children's parties or other celebrations. We used a combination of zingy hot pinks and oranges, but you could try making paper chains in soft pastel tones or in red and white for Christmas decorations.

YOU WILL NEED:

selection of colored paper at least 12 inches (30 cm) wide • pencil • ruler • scissors • glue

choose colors Ask your child what colors she or he would like to use to create the chains. For more decorative paper chains, you could use patterned wrapping paper or translucent tracing paper, which is available from art stores in a variety of different colors.

draw strips Using a pencil and ruler, draw the strips on the back of the paper, making sure that each one is approximately 1 inch (2.5 cm) wide.

cut strips Using scissors, cut out the strips. It is a good idea to keep the colors separate by making a pile of strips in each color, so they are easier to select when joining the chains together.

glue strips into chains Form a loop with the first paper chain and put a dab of glue on one end to fix it together. For the next link in the chain, thread the paper through the loop and glue the ends. Repeat for each link until you have made the length of paper chain you want.

Use pretty handmade paper to cover textbooks or notebooks. You can use them at school or give them as gifts. The same technique can be used to decorate boxes or photo albums, which make welcome keepsakes.

covering books

cut out paper Lay the book out flat on the paper to be used to cover it. Cut around the book, leaving a margin of about 1½ inches (4 cm) of extra paper around all the sides. Where the spine of the book lies, cut two slits in the paper at the top and bottom of the book, and fold them inwards to hide them.

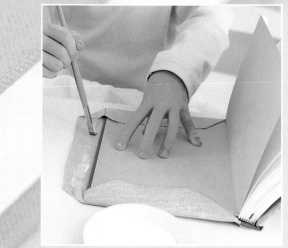

glue on cover Fold the remaining edges of the paper toward the inside of the book and make pleated folds at the corners to neaten the edges. Glue the paper to the book and let dry completely. It is a good idea to glue each layer of paper at the folded corners so that they stay in place.

cut out decorations Use scissors to cut out a selection of flowers, petals, and whatever other decorations are desired. These can be drawn using a pencil first, or cut out freehand, depending upon the child.

decorate Lay out the paper shapes on the book to create the design. When you are happy with the arrangement, glue each piece in place. If the pieces are very small, it is a good idea to use a fine paintbrush to apply the glue to the back of the paper. Let dry thoroughly.

gift boxes

Use ready-made gift boxes or recycle chocolate and biscuit boxes to create these pretty gifts. Cover the boxes in paper, then cut out heart and flower petals in contrasting colors and differently textured paper to decorate the box with. If you like, you could use the template for a paper flower given on page 118.

photo album

The album cover is made from two stiff pieces of card stock covered in paper. The word "PHOTOS" and a paper flower were glued to the front. Place paper between the covers and use a hole punch to make holes through the covers and paper. Thread with stretchy string to hold the album together.

books

Decorative flowers, or narrow strips of colored paper glued in horizontal bands, look great on paper-covered books. Boys can decorate their books with boats, trains, or car shapes cut from brightly colored papers.

little tips

Remember that the thinner the paper, the easier it will be to cover items. Thick handmade paper can be quite difficult to fold, particularly at the corners. It's best to save thicker handmade papers for the decorations, as they will be easier to glue to the flat surfaces of the objects.

Like paper chains, paper lanterns are a traditional and fun way of using paper to make three-dimensional objects. They look great strung across a window or mantelpiece. We decorated ours with bands of gingham ribbon, but you could substitute buttons, sequins, or glitter.

paper lanterns

YOU WILL NEED:
sheets of letter-sized paper in various colors • scissors • glue • ribbon for decorating

cut and fold paper
Cut a strip of paper about ½-inch (1-cm) wide from the shortest side of the piece of paper and set aside. This will make the hanging loop. Now, cut a square 8 x 8 inches (20 x 20 cm). Fold the square in half and press flat.

cut equal strips
Cutting inwards from the folded edge of the paper, use scissors to snip flaps that finish about 1¼ inches (3 cm) from the top of the paper. Each flap should be spaced about ¾ inch (2 cm) apart. You may want to mark the lines out using a pencil and a ruler first, to make it easier for the child to cut the paper properly.

glue into a round
To make the lantern shape, unfold the creased edge and roll the paper to form a tube shape with the paper slits standing vertically. Glue the edges of the paper together to form a round lantern, then press downwards gently to form a splayed lantern shape.

finish off
Cut a piece of ribbon to fit around the top of the lantern and glue it in place. Glue the ends of the hanging loop to the top of the lantern on both sides, and let dry completely.

This very effective paper technique will provide children with hours of pleasure and can be adapted to suit most ages. Collect wrapping paper, paper doilies, newspapers, and magazine cuttings, and keep them in a découpage box. You can also buy books of découpage scraps.

découpage

YOU WILL NEED:
box for covering • assorted
papers in different sizes •
glue • scissors

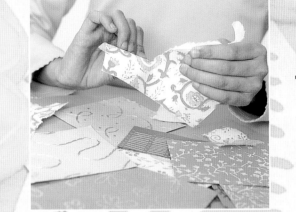

tear and cut materials

Découpage looks particularly effective when both cut and torn pieces of paper are used—the ragged edges add to the layered effect. For added interest, you could also try using decorative scissors and pinking shears to cut some of the paper.

glue on Start by sticking larger pieces of paper onto the box to cover it completely. This saves time and provides a good background for the smaller pieces of paper that are added later. Always let the glue dry thoroughly before embarking on the next layer of paper.

layer upon layer When the first layer is dry, add more smaller pieces of paper. We used torn pieces of paper as well as smaller squares to cover the box. Try to allow some drying time between layers, so that the wet glue does not cause the layer beneath to peel away.

finish off Finish the découpage with smaller shapes such as flowers or leaves cut from wrapping paper. It may be easier to use a fine paintbrush to apply the glue to these smaller, more fiddly pieces of paper.

toy box

Simple black-and-white designs look particularly effective in découpage. This toy-box was made from an old shoe box, and has been covered with designs of antique playing cards photocopied from a non-copyright book on the subject.

craft kit

Layers of handmade papers decorated with floral and metallic designs were used to cover this craft kit box. Individual flowers and leaf shapes were cut out to finish off the découpage design.

bon-bon box

Layers of handmade paper and roses cut from scraps of vintage-style wallpaper were used to cover a heart-shaped box, which was then filled with candies to create a pretty gift for a friend or relative. The edges are trimmed with paper lace cut from the edge of a rectangular doily and finished with a border of thin velvet ribbon.

little tips

Découpage is traditionally finished with layers of varnish to make the object more durable. A few layers of water-based acrylic varnish is ideal, but make sure that it is applied in thin layers to prevent saturating the paper, which could peel off. Let the varnish dry thoroughly between each coat.

modeling

papier mâché dinosaur

Papier mâché is a really hands-on messy project, so make sure you have enough time to get the materials ready and to clear up afterwards! Kids love working with papier mâché due to its sloshy consistency and the fact it can be used to create fantastic three-dimensional objects.

YOU WILL NEED:
newspaper • balloon • bowl to support balloon • thick brushes • white glue • bowl for glue • aluminum foil for the dinosaur's legs and head • cardboard (we used the back of a hard-backed envelope) • paint • masking tape

cover balloon Tear the newspaper into strips and put aside. Blow up the balloon and balance it on a bowl while you stick on the paper. Using a brush, apply glue to the balloon. Cover with paper. Repeat the process, building up layers of paper, until the balloon is thickly covered.

add legs and head We used ordinary aluminum foil rolled into short cylinder shapes for the legs and head. Use masking tape to attach them to the balloon. Apply glue to the legs and head, and cover with strips of paper. Make sure that the strips overlap onto the body so that the head and legs will be securely held in place once the glue has dried.

add spines Cut out triangles from the cardboard measuring ¾ inch (2 cm) wide and 1½ inches (4 cm) high. Fold the bottom of the triangle and glue the flat part to the balloon. Form two lines to create the dinosaur's spikes. When dry, apply another layer of paper to hold the spikes in place.

finish off Once the glue is dry, the dinosaur is ready to paint. It is best to leave the papier mâché overnight to make sure all the layers are dry. Paint the dinosaur body in mauve and the spikes in bright blue. Let the paint dry completely. We added blue spots to the body to finish off.

glue base

For the bottom of the boat, cut seven pieces of balsa wood measuring 4 x ½ x ½ inch (10 x 1 x 1 cm). Lay two pieces of the wood parallel about 3½ inches (9 cm) apart, and glue the other five pieces across them on the top at equal intervals. For the mast, cut two cubes of wood measuring ½ x ½ inch (1 x 1 cm) and two lengths measuring 4 inches (10 cm) long and ¼ inch (5 mm) square.

paint bottom

Paint the base of the boat and the mast sections and let them dry completely. You may need to apply another coat of paint to ensure even coverage. Let the paint dry completely before attaching the mast.

make sail and mast

Cut out a triangle of fabric about 3¼ x 3¼ inches (8 x 8 cm) square, using pinking shears to prevent the fabric from fraying. Lay one mast piece on the table and apply glue down the center of the fabric triangle before placing it on the mast. Lay the second mast on top, so the sail is neatly sandwiched between the pieces of wood, then glue it in place. Let it dry.

attach sail

Glue the bottom of the mast to the two cubes of balsa wood so that it is held between them. Now apply a blob of glue to the center of the bottom of the boat, and stick the sail and mast to it. Let the glue dry. You may wish to apply more paint to cover the glue in this area.

Balsa wood is easy to cut and glue, which makes it ideal for children to use for modeling. Small pieces can be cut with scissors, but thicker pieces of balsa wood should be cut by an adult using a junior hacksaw.

modeling with balsa wood

sailing ship

This fun sailing ship was made
using the technique shown on
pages 78–79. Children will have
hours of fun sailing their ships in
buckets, the bathtub, or even a
local pond, but do remember to
attach a piece of string if you're
sailing the boat outdoors, so that
it can't float away!

doll's table and chairs

You'll need a piece of balsa wood measuring 2½ x 4 inches (6 x 10 cm) for the top of the table, and four legs made from ½-inch (1-cm) square balsa wood cut into 1½ inch (4 cm) lengths. The chair seats and legs were made from balsa, while the ladder-style backs were made from popsicle sticks. We painted the table blue and added a decorative motif in red to match the chairs.

doll's bed

A delightful addition to any little girl's doll's house, this bed is made from a piece of balsa measuring about 4 x 2½ inches (10 x 6 cm) wide. The back was cut from a thin piece of balsa wood and the legs are four ½-inch (1-cm) square pieces of balsa wood. The bed was painted red and decorated with a Shaker-style motif in white, done using a fine paintbrush. The quilt was made from two rectangles of gingham fabric trimmed with a piece of ribbon.

little tips

If you're working with young children, it's advisable to cut the pieces of balsa wood for them. Any rough edges should be lightly sanded with sandpaper to smooth them off. Having pre-cut pieces of balsa means that the kids can move on quickly to the fun bits of the project—the glueing and painting!

Snow globes make great gifts for friends and family, and children really enjoy making them. We used Christmas decorations inside ours, but your child may like to use small plastic animals or to make their own decorations to put inside.

snow globes

YOU WILL NEED:
empty, clean jam jars • distilled water • glycerin • liquid dish detergent • pitcher and spoon for pouring • glitter • Christmas decorations to put in jar • strong waterproof glue

fill jars Use a pitcher to pour the distilled water into the jam jar. Fill it as full as possible. Add two teaspoons of glycerin, and half a teaspoon of dish detergent.

add glitter Spoon the glitter into the water. You will need about five or six teaspoons. White or silver glitter looks most similar to snow, although red or green or other bright colors can look very festive.

attach decoration Use a blob of strong waterproof glue to securely stick the decoration to the inside of the jam-jar lid. It is advisable for an adult to do this if the child is young. Let the glue dry thoroughly according to the manufacturer's instructions.

secure lid Carefully place the lid on the top of the jam jar and screw tightly in place. The jam jar should be watertight, but you may wish to seal it around the edges with a layer of craft silicone sealant, which is available from good craft stores.

YOU WILL NEED:
air-drying modeling clay • rolling
pin • assorted cookie cutters •
spatula • paint dish or saucer •
paintbrushes • paints • glue •
loose sequins • tweezers •
drinking straw • self-adhesive
magnets • ribbon for necklaces •
metal pins for brooches

roll out Remove the clay from
its packaging and knead to soften it.
Roll the clay out with a rolling pin.
For smaller objects such as
brooches, the clay should be about
¼ inch (5 mm) thick. For larger
objects, the clay should be about
⅜ inch (8 mm) thick.

cut out Use assorted cookie cutters to cut the shapes from
the clay. Carefully remove the excess clay from around the
cutter before removing it. Use a spatula to lift the clay shape
and place it on a tray for it to dry. When the top is dry, turn
the shape over so the other side can dry completely.

paint and decorate Paint your clay shapes using brightly colored
paints. You will probably need two or three layers of paint to achieve total
coverage, but remember to let each layer dry thoroughly between coats.
Paler colors may need more coats than darker shades.

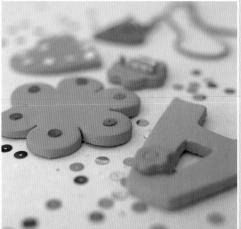

finish off Decorate the finished clay
shapes with sequins or smaller clay
shapes using a tiny bit of glue. You may
need tweezers to position sequins on
the shapes. Stick magnets to the back
for fridge magnets, and metal pins to
make brooches. Use self-adhesive pads
to stick the letters to a door.

Children love working with clay, and it can be used to create fun jewelry for friends, alphabet letters for doors, and funky fridge magnets. Nowadays, metal or plastic cookie cutters come in all sorts of shapes and sizes, and will cut clay quickly and easily. Once dry, your clay shapes can be colorfully painted and decorated.

modeling with clay

letter shapes

Children will love cutting out their names in clay letters and sticking them on their bedroom doors. We decorated these letters with tiny flowers, using a miniature cutter for the flower shape and a straw to imprint the central circle in the flower. Paint the letters in bold colors and use self-adhesive pads to attach them to the door. They can also be used to decorate toy boxes and wooden trunks.

jewelry

Little girls will enjoy creating jewelry for themselves and their friends. Use small cookie-cutter shapes such as flowers and hearts and roll out the clay to ¼ inch (5 mm) thick, so the shapes are not too heavy. Use a straw to pierce a ribbon hole for necklaces. Paint the shapes in bright colors and decorate with sequins.

fridge magnets

Cookie cutters in the shape of fish, flowers, and butterflies can be used to create fun fridge magnets. Paint them in pretty colors and decorate with sequins. Alternatively, use different colored paint to decorate. Most craft stores now sell self-adhesive magnets that can be bought in strips and cut to size.

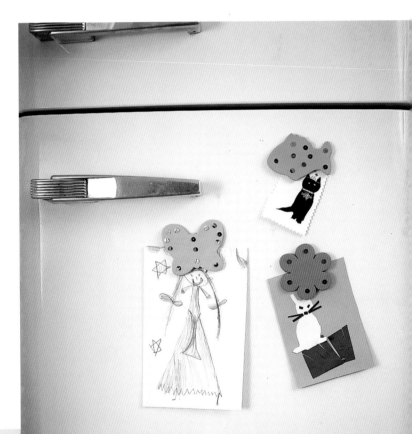

little tips

Avoid putting the clay near water, as it will make it sticky and difficult to use • Keep left-over clay wrapped in plastic or in an airtight container for future use • A couple of coats of varnish (applied by an adult) will give the painted clay a longer life.

These classic puppet people have been made by children for years and will provide hours of entertainment. Their outfits are made from semicircles of fabric or paper, while string or wool is used for the hair. We used a large cardboard box covered in wrapping paper to create the puppet theater.

wooden-spoon puppets

YOU WILL NEED:

wooden spoons • black pen • scissors • string or wool • glue • 12-inch (30-cm) dinner plate as template for clothes • pinking shears • cotton fabric, felt, or paper doilies for clothes • buttons, ribbons, and small silk flowers for decoration

making faces

Use a fine liner pen to draw the faces onto the wooden spoons. Let the child use his or her imagination and add rosy cheeks, noses, and eyebrows with colored pencils if they want to.

adding the hair

For braided hair with bangs, cut six pieces of string or wool measuring about 12 inches (30 cm) and two pieces measuring 3¼ inches (8 cm). Knot the shorter pieces of string in the middle of the longer pieces to create the effect of bangs. Alternatively, use ten 12-inch (30-cm) pieces for long loose hair, and six shorter 2½ inch (6 cm) pieces for the boy puppet's hair. Neatly glue the hair to the top of the wooden spoons.

dressing up

Use a 12-inch (30-cm) dinner plate as a template. Place it on your chosen fabric and draw around the edge using black pen. Cut each circle out, then cut into two halves to create semicircular shapes. Use pinking shears to prevent fabric from fraying. Wrap the fabric around the neck of the spoon and glue it in place. Add little buttons or ribbons to decorate.

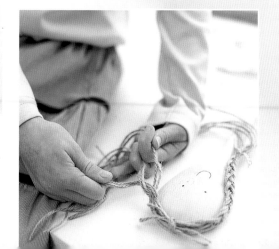

finish off

Carefully braid the doll's hair and tie the ends with short pieces of colorful ribbon.

Hanging mobiles are a fun project for boys and girls, and make decorative additions to any bedroom. They are also a lovely present for a new baby. A great variety of materials can be used to make mobiles, from wire and beads to balsa wood and modeling clay.

hanging mobiles

YOU WILL NEED:

wire for the hearts • thinner wire for attaching hearts to mobile • colored beads • bell for decoration • scissors • two pieces of balsa wood, about 12 inches (30 cm) long • paint for mobile frame • glue

thread beads on wire

Thread the wooden beads onto the wire, alternating the colors for a pretty effect. We used twenty-seven beads for each wired heart.

shape into heart Place the beaded wire onto a flat surface and bend the wire to form the heart shape. Your child may need a little help in doing this, especially when it comes to forming the loop at the center.

form loop and make frame Bend the wire to form a loop in the center of the heart shape and twist the wire to secure it. Thread the bell onto thin wire and attach to the loop by twisting it around the wire. Now paint the two pieces of balsa wood for the frame. Place one piece on top of the other to form a cross shape, and glue in position.

attach to frame Cut four 12-inch (30 cm) pieces of thin wire and thread one onto each of the heart loops. Twist one end to secure it to the loop, then twist the other end around one end of the frame. Repeat with the three other hearts.

cars

Balsa wood is ideal for mobiles, as it is very lightweight and can be easily cut into interesting shapes. For this mobile, we drew little car shapes, wheel shapes, and window shapes on thin balsa wood, and then cut them out. Paint the cars and windows in bright colors and use black for the wheels. When the paint is dry, glue the windows and wheels onto the car outlines. Make a small hole at the top of each car and thread thin wire through the hole so that it can be attached to the frame.

beaded hearts

This beaded mobile was made using the technique shown on pages 90–91. Threading beads is great for helping children develop their fine motor skills. Younger children who find small beads too fiddly could thread larger beads or painted pasta tubes on shoelaces and suspend them from a mobile frame.

pretty purple flowers

Use a cookie cutter to cut out flower shapes from thinly rolled-out modeling clay, and a drinking straw to cut out a hole to hang them from. Paint the flower shapes both back and front and let them dry. Then add spots in a contrasting color. Thread narrow ribbon through each hole and tie a bow. Attach a piece of narrow wire to each flower shape, and hang it from the mobile frame.

little tips

Look out for small wooden toys or even tiny soft toys to suspend from mobiles for babies • Monochromatic designs in black and white are visually appealing to very young babies, so you could paint bold patterns on clay or wood shapes and paint the bars of the mobile in narrow black and white stripes.

special
occasions

Clothes-peg dolls are a traditional craft. They are the perfect size for doll's houses and can be dressed as men or women. Clothes-peg dolls look cute dressed as Christmas angels in white lace with silver wings, or as Santa Claus in red felt with a cotton-ball beard.

clothes-peg angels

YOU WILL NEED:
wooden clothes-pegs • black
pen for face and silver pen for
shoes • scraps of lace and
cotton for dress • scissors •
glue • pipe-cleaner for halo •
silver card stock for wings •
sheer ribbon for hanging loop

draw on face and feet

Use the black pen to draw some eyes and mouth on the clothes-peg. Color in the feet to look like shoes using the silver felt-tip pen, and let dry.

cut out and glue robes
Cut a piece of white cotton and a piece of lace both measuring 3¼ x 3¼ inches (8 x 8 cm). Lay the white cotton on top of the lace and glue one end of the fabric to the back of the peg doll. Wrap the other layer of fabric around the doll and glue at the back.

attach wings
Using scissors, carefully cut a pair of small wings from the silver card stock. Apply a dab of glue to the wings, and stick them into place on the back of the clothes-peg doll.

add halo and ribbon
Twist the pipe cleaner into a circular shape to form a halo, and place it on the clothes-peg doll's head. Cut a piece of sheer ribbon about 8 inches (20 cm) long and tie it around the doll's neck. Tie the two ends of the ribbon into a knot to form a hanging loop.

YOU WILL NEED:
paper • pencil • scissors

fold paper Take a square piece of paper. Fold it in half diagonally. Fold the paper in half again, and then into quarters. You should now have a small folded paper triangle.

draw on design Using the pencil, draw triangular or scalloped shapes on the folded edges of the paper. You can draw curved shapes on the top edges of the paper (furthest from the center of the paper), too. Experiment with different shapes, so that all your snowflakes are different.

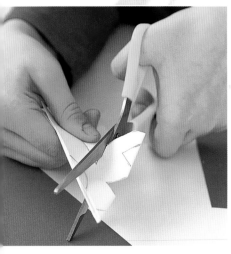

cut out Using the scissors, carefully cut along the lines you have drawn on the paper. Remember that the more shapes you cut out, the more decorative and delicate the snowflake will appear.

pull open Gently unfold the paper and carefully press flat to reveal the snowflake's design. You can cut snowflakes from any size paper, but good sizes are about 8 inches (20 cm) square for a large snowflake and 4 inches (10 cm) square for a small one.

paper snowflakes

Paper snowflakes are so simple to make, yet so effective. At Christmas, use them to decorate windows, stick them to the wall in a circular shape to create a wreath effect, or hang them from bare branches as a tabletop decoration. Snip them from white paper, tissue paper, or tracing paper. We used both red and white paper for our festive display.

Decorate simple cones of card stock with sequins, glitter, and pompoms to create pretty tree-top angels. Feathers or leaf skeletons, which are available from art stores, make great wings. Alternatively, create a tree-top Santa Claus with red felt and a cotton-ball beard, or Rudolf the reindeer using brown card stock and pipe cleaner antlers.

tree toppers

YOU WILL NEED:

white card stock • 12-inch (30-cm) dinner plate for template • sequin trim • small white pompom • feathers for wings • glue • stapler, if necessary • scissors • pencil • silver pipe cleaner for halo

apply sequin border

Use the 12-inch (30-cm) plate to draw out a semicircle on the card stock. Cut out with scissors. Glue the sequin trim around the curved edge of the semicircle, about ½ inch (1 cm) from the edge. Let dry.

form the body Roll the card to form a cone shape. Glue the edges in place and let dry. You may want to staple the join as well, to make the cone more secure.

glue on pompom head Put a dab of glue on a pompom and attach it to the top of the cone. Use a silver pipe cleaner to form a circular halo to fit on top of the pompom, and use a small amount of glue to hold it in place.

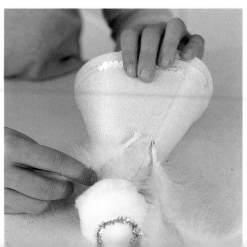

attach wings Use glue to attach the feathers at the back of the cone for the angel's wings. We used two white feathers for each wing. Allow the glue to dry completely.

A simple cone of black card stock is the basis of this spooky witch's hat with a brim, or the simpler wizard's hat without a brim. Decorate with black net and silver stars for a night of trick or treating!

halloween hat

YOU WILL NEED:

black card stock • pencil • scissors • stapler or strong sticky tape (e.g. duct tape) • star-shaped cookie cutter to use as template • silver paper for stars • glue • black netting

measure and cut Cut out a semicircle of black card stock with a diameter of about 24 inches (60 cm). Roll into a cone shape and fit to the child's head. Mark out the line where the card should be joined. Use strong tape to create the cone (we used black duct tape, which is the same color as the hat). A couple of staples will make the hat more secure.

cut out brim Place the cone on a sheet of black card stock and draw all the way around the opening. Then draw another larger circle about 3¼ inches (8 cm) wider, to form the brim. Mark out a smaller circle ¾ inch (2 cm) within the inner circle to allow for the flaps for the brim. Cut out the brim from the card stock. Use scissors to cut the flaps for the brim at intervals of ¾ inch (2 cm) all around the inner circle.

attach hat and brim Fold alternate flaps back and sit the cone on top of the brim. Use strong sticky duct tape to fix the flaps to the cone. Make sure that the tape is firmly pressed down to keep the brim in place.

decorate We used a star-shaped cookie cutter as a template to draw stars on silver paper. Cut them out with scissors and glue carefully to the hat. We also added a piece of black netting, which we glued to the point of the hat as a finishing touch.

This fun cat mask is perfect for Halloween or a dress-up party. Black is the best choice for Halloween, but it would look equally cute in brown or white. Add some pipe cleaner whiskers and a little pompom for the cat's nose.

cat mask

YOU WILL NEED:
tracing paper • black card stock • black felt • glue • scissors • pompom for nose • pipe-cleaners for whiskers • hole punch • piece of elastic

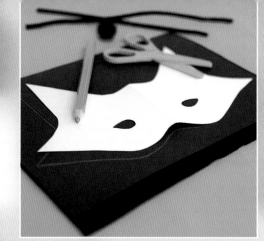

draw templates Trace the mask template on page 119 onto a piece of folded paper and cut it out. Open out the template. Take the piece of black felt and glue it to the piece of black card stock. Let it dry.

cut out mask Draw around the paper template on the card side of the glued card and felt. Carefully cut out with scissors, taking particular care when cutting out the eye holes. An adult may need to help by first making a slit in the card stock for the eyes, so that the scissors can be easily inserted for cutting.

attach nose and whiskers Glue the pompom nose onto the mask. Cut six pipe-cleaner whiskers measuring about 4 inches (10 cm) long, and glue them to each side of the mask, just below the eye holes. Let dry.

attach elastic band Using a hole punch, make a hole on each side of the mask in the position indicated on the template. Thread one end of the elastic through a hole and knot it to secure. Thread the elastic through the other hole, tie a knot, and trim any excess elastic to finish.

YOU WILL NEED:
white paper bag • scissors • pencil • round paper doily • glue • brushes for glue • pastel-colored cupcake cups • stapler • hole punch • ribbon for ties, about 1 inch (2.5 cm) wide

cut paper bag
Cut off the top edge of the paper bag, so that the height of the bag is about 8 inches (20 cm). Draw a curve all the way from one bottom corner of the bag to the top, leaving the gusset edges of the bag flat.

glue on trim
Cut the curved edges of the paper doily about 1½ inches (4 cm) wide. Cut another piece of doily with a straight edge to fit the gusset edge of the bag. Glue the doily to the inside of the hat along the curved edges and the straight top edge, and let dry completely.

create rosettes
Open up the paper cupcake cups and carefully flatten them out. Fold each one in quarters to create a rosette shape, and attach two or three of them to one side of the bonnet using a stapler. Fluff out the rosettes once they are attached, so that they look like flowers.

finish off
Using a hole punch, make a hole on either side of the hat near the bottom of the curved edge. Thread one end of the ribbon through one hole and knot it to secure it. Take the other end of the ribbon, thread it through the second hole, and tie a knot to hold it in place.

easter bonnet

This cute bonnet is made from a plain paper bag decorated with the edge of a paper doily, while the delicate rosettes are made from paper cupcake cups. It is the perfect project for little girls to create for an Easter bonnet competition.

Real eggs painted in soft pastel colors and tied with sheer organza ribbons make a simple but effective display for Easter. Older children may like to blow the eggs first, but it is easier simply to boil them before painting and decorating.

painted eggs

YOU WILL NEED:
eggs • assorted pastel-colored paints • selection of fine paintbrushes • egg cartons or eggcups to hold eggs for painting • sheer ribbon, about ½ inch (1 cm) wide

take the eggs Select the eggs and boil the number you want for decorating. Let the eggs cool completely before you start decorating them. You may like to cut up egg cartons to hold the eggs while you are painting them.

paint eggs Paint the eggs in the chosen base color and let them to dry completely. You may need to apply a second coat for complete coverage. Let dry before adding any additional decoration.

add decoration Use a fine paintbrush to add dots, swirls, and stripes in a contrasting colored paint and let it dry thoroughly. It is easier to paint one half of the egg first, and then let it dry before completing the other side, to prevent the paint from smudging.

finish off Cut pieces of sheer ribbon and tie one around each egg, finishing with a bow. Group the eggs nestled together in a bowl or on a glass cake stand to create a decorative Easter display.

mother's day gift

This delicate bowl uses the traditional papier mâché technique combined with white glue and plastic wrap, which means that the bowl can be created with fewer layers of paper for a more delicate appearance.

YOU WILL NEED:
bowl or plate to use as mold •
plastic wrap • newspaper •
white glue • bowl for glue •
thick brushes for glue • paints
in your chosen colors •
assorted brushes for painting •
scissors

cover bowl Place the bowl mold upside-down on a flat surface and cover with a layer of plastic wrap. Tear the newspaper into strips. Paint over the plastic wrap with a layer of white glue, then apply the first layer of paper. Repeat the process until you have built up four layers of paper. Let dry overnight.

lift off papier mâché bowl When it is completely dry, gently ease the papier mâché bowl away from the ceramic bowl and remove the plastic wrap. You can tidy the edges of the bowl with scissors, if you like.

paint the bowl Using a thick paintbrush, paint the bowl inside and out with the main color. Let dry, then apply a second coat of paint. Let dry before applying the decoration to the bowl.

decorate We decorated the bowl with lilac and pink daisies both inside and out. You may find it easier to draw the design on the bowl in pencil first, before applying the paint. Let it dry. A coat of water-based acrylic varnish will seal the paint and give a more hard-wearing finish.

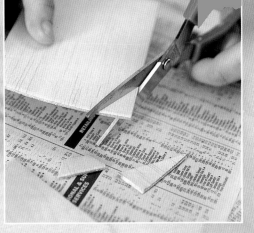

YOU WILL NEED:

thin wood sheet (available from craft stores) • balsa wood • pencil • scissors • paint in your chosen colors • saucer to hold paints • paintbrushes in various sizes • glue • keyring attachment • bradawl

cut simple shapes
Cut small rectangles from the wood sheet. This will be the base of the keyring. Now draw simple motifs straight onto the balsa wood and cut them out using scissors. An adult may need to assist a younger child in cutting the wood.

paint base and cutouts
Paint the base of the keyring all over the back and front and let it dry. A second coat of paint may be necessary for even coverage. Paint the front and edges of the smaller balsa-wood pieces using a fine paintbrush. Let dry.

glue on motif
Apply glue to the back of the balsa-wood pieces and stick them in place on the front of the keyring. Press down firmly. Let the glue dry completely. You may wish to apply a coat of water-based acrylic varnish to make the keyring more hard-wearing.

attach chain
Make a small hole at the top of the keyring using a bradawl (similar to a screwdriver, but with a sharp point at the end). For safety reasons, it is advisable for an adult to do this part of the project. Take the keyring attachment, thread the metal loop through the hole, and close it with pliers.

These decorative keyrings are made from balsa wood and thin wood sheets, and make the perfect gift for Father's Day. Key chains are available from craft stores and are easily attached to the wood. Both boys and girls will love this easy woodwork technique.

father's day gift

valentine's day card

This three-dimensional Valentine's Day card features hearts made from decorative handmade paper. Tissue paper and paper doilies would also make pretty hearts for the card. Use pinking shears and decorative scissors (available from craft stores) to cut the paper, and finish with a ribbon bow.

YOU WILL NEED:
selection of decorative paper (scraps of wrapping paper are ideal) • blank greeting cards (or card stock folded in half) • pinking shears or decorative cutting scissors • glue • ribbon for bows • pencil • plain paper for template

draw hearts For the card, you need three heart shapes in decreasing sizes. Fold the decorative papers in half and press the crease flat. Draw half a heart shape in three different sizes onto three different pieces of decorative paper.

cut out hearts Use the decorative cutting scissors or pinking shears to cut around the edges of the heart motif and open it out flat. Cut out the two smaller heart shapes in the same way. If you wish, you can cut out more hearts in graduating sizes to make an even more decorative card.

layer hearts Apply a line of glue down the center of the back of the largest heart, stick it to the middle of the card, and press it flat. Apply glue to the center back of the smaller heart and glue it to the first heart shape on the card. Attach the smallest heart in the same way. Let the glue dry.

finish off Using sheer organza or velvet ribbon, cut a bow and trim the ends diagonally to prevent the ribbon from fraying. Apply a small dot of glue to the central knot of the bow and stick to the heart. Let it dry. A matching ribbon looks pretty stuck to the back of the envelope flap, too.

YOU WILL NEED:
flowers and leaves • flower press • glue • brushes for glue • object for decoration (bookmark, picture frame, or greetings card) • tweezers for lifting flowers, if necessary

choose flowers
It is fun to pick flowers from the garden, but if this is not possible use store-bought flowers. The flatter the flower, the easier it is to press. If the flower is bulky, pull off the petals, press them individually, and use them to recreate the flower once they are pressed.

press flowers
Carefully place the flowers and leaves in the press between the layers of paper and card. Replace the top of the flower press and tighten the screws as firmly as you can. This ensures that as little air as possible can get to the flowers and leaves. An adult may need to help with tightening the screws.

remove flowers from press
The flowers and leaves should be left for about a week to make sure they are completely dry. Once dry, peel them away from the papers in the press as carefully as possible, since they become fragile once they're dry. Place them on a sheet of paper ready for application.

apply to desired object
Apply a thin layer of glue to the back of a flower. Gently lift the flower and place it in position (use tweezers if you want to). Add other flowers until the design is complete. Let it dry thoroughly. If decorating a box, apply a layer of water-based acrylic varnish.

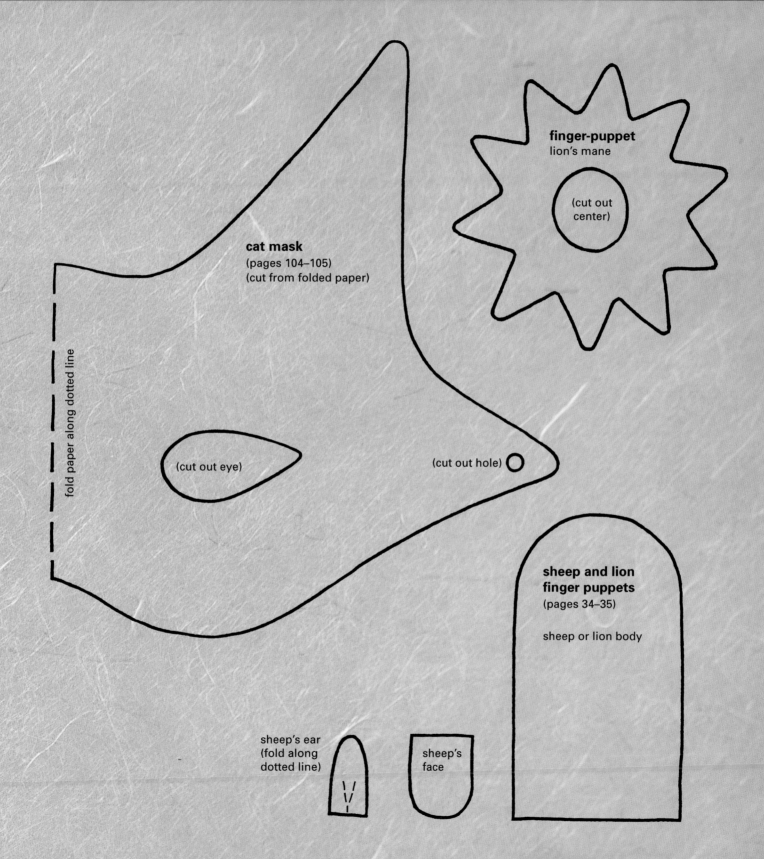

finger-puppet
lion's mane

(cut out center)

cat mask
(pages 104–105)
(cut from folded paper)

fold paper along dotted line

(cut out eye)

(cut out hole)

sheep and lion finger puppets
(pages 34–35)

sheep or lion body

sheep's ear
(fold along dotted line)

sheep's face

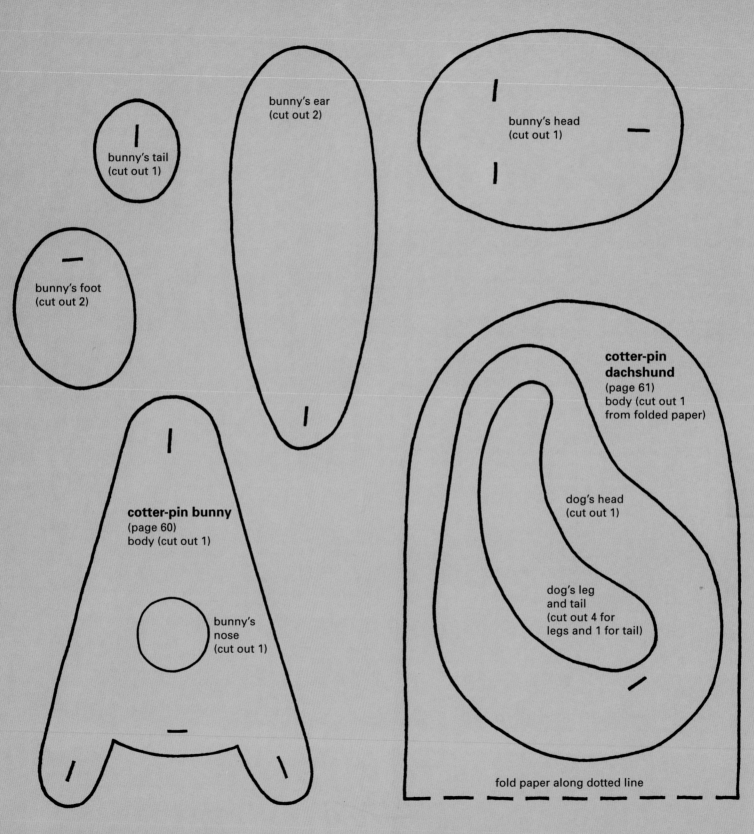

bunny's tail
(cut out 1)

bunny's ear
(cut out 2)

bunny's head
(cut out 1)

bunny's foot
(cut out 2)

**cotter-pin
dachshund**
(page 61)
body (cut out 1
from folded paper)

dog's head
(cut out 1)

cotter-pin bunny
(page 60)
body (cut out 1)

bunny's
nose
(cut out 1)

dog's leg
and tail
(cut out 4 for
legs and 1 for tail)

fold paper along dotted line

cotter-pin teddy
(pages 58–59)

teddy's body
(cut out 1)

teddy's nose
(cut out 1)

teddy oval
(cut out 2 for ears,
4 for arms and
6 for legs and feet)

teddy's head
(cut out 1)

dachshund's ear
(cut out 1)

dog's eye
and nose
(cut out 1
for each)

sources

A. C. Moore
Visit www.acmoore.com for details of your nearest store. *Chain of craft superstores. Visit their website for some fun craft projects for kids.*

The Baker's Kitchen
3326 Glanzman Rd.
Toledo, OH 43614
419-381-9693
www.thebakerskitchen.com
Cake decorating, candy making, baking and kitchen supplies. Decorative doilies, baking cups, and a large range of cookie cutters in novel shapes.

Britex Fabrics
146 Geary Street
San Francisco, CA 94108
415-392-2910
www.britexfabrics.com
Wide variety of pretty ribbons, trims, and notions that are great for adding a finishing touch.

The Button Emporium & Ribbonry
914 S.W. 11th Avenue
Portland, OR 97205
503-228-6372
www.buttonemporium.com
Vintage and assorted buttons and ribbons. Also some jewelry findings.

Candyland Crafts
201 W. Main Street
Somerville, NJ 08876
908-685-0410
www.candylandcrafts.com
Baking and muffin cups, cupcake display stands, novelty cookie cutters, edible cake decorations, fondant icing, and sugar paste.

Crafting Direct
www.craftingdirect.com
All kinds of essential crafting equipment for kids: cards and papers, glitter and white glue, metallic tape, découpage kits, plastic stencils, ready-pressed flowers, bumper packs of sequins and beads, and more.

Dick Blick Art Materials
Locations throughout the Midwest. Visit www.dickblick.com for details of your nearest store.
A Dick Blick store is an Aladdin's cave of art and craft supplies. They carry air-drying clay, balsa wood, cold-water fabric dyes, jewelry finding, adhesive magnets, fabaric paint and stencilling equipment, wooden clothes-pegs, felt, and cutting tools such as pinking shears.

Discount School Supplies
www.discountschoolsupplies.com
Arts and crafts materials for early learners. Colored pipe cleaners, wooden craft sticks, and ready-made pompoms.

Hobby Lobby
Locations nationwide.
Call 405-745-1100 or visit www.hobbylobby.com for details of your nearest store.
Discount arts and crafts stores. Find suggestions for kids' crafts on their website.

Hyman Hendler & Sons
67 West 38th Street
New York, NY 10018
212-840-8393
www.hymanhendler.com
Their speciality is novelty and vintage ribbons in many different colors and designs.

JAM Paper
Call 800-8010-JAM or visit www.jampaper.com for details of your nearest store.
Papers of all sizes and customized rubber stamps.

JoAnn Fabrics
Locations nationwide.
Visit www.joann.com for details of your nearest store.
Art and crafts supplier offering a wide selection of paper, cards, craft materials, fabric, scrapbooking materials, and more.

Kate's Paperie
561 Broadway
New York, NY 10012
212-941-9816
888-809-9880
www.katespaperie.com
Kate's Paperie carries over 40,000 exotic papers from around the world. Also stickers, stamps, paper punches, and ribbons.

Loose Ends
2065 Madrona Ave. SE
Salem, OR 97302
www.looseends.com
Craft materials including dried flowers and foliage, glues and adhesives, gift wrap, collage materials, plain papier-mâché forms to decorate, many different ribbons and ties, and more.

Michaels
Locations nationwide.
Visit www.michaels.com for details of your nearest store.
A huge selection of every kind of art and craft material. They have special areas for kids' products, including air-drying clay, easy sewing kits, plain keepsake boxes to decorate, collage materials, Makit & Bakit® ceramic painting kits, and essential basics like glue and paint.

M&J Trimming
www.mjtrim.com
Amazing selection of rhinestones, crocheted appliqués, sequined flowers, ribbons, lace, rosettes, beaded braid, and fur and feather trims, all available to buy online.

New York Cake Supplies
56 West 22nd Street
New York, NY 10010
800-942-2539
www.nycake.com
Bakeware, rolling pins, and a large selection of novelty cookie cutters that are ideal for cutting clay shapes

Oriental Trading Co.
1-800-875-8480
www.orientaltrading.com
Art and craft supplies, embellishments, and some fun ready-made craft kits. They also carry a wide selection of jewelry-making equipment, including tools, jewelry findings, and assorted beads.

Paper Creations
425 Water Street
Appleton, WI 54911-6058
920-734-6871
www.papercreations.com
Papercrafting, scrapbooking supplies, and many different rubber stamps. Good for card stock and blank greetings cards and envelopes in different colors.

Paper Source
www.paper-source.com
Simple, stylish crafting kits for mother's day presents as well as many other special occasions. Also envelopes, cards, and pretty handmade paper in a variety of designs, as well as crafting basics such as scissors, glue, and hole punches.

Paper Wishes
888-300-3406
www.paperwishes.com
Good for card-making equipment, different kinds of paper, scrapbooks, stamps and stamping accessories, stickers, tools, and more.

Pearl Art and Crafts Supplies
225 W Chicago Ave
Chicago, IL 60610
www.pearlpaint.com
Discount art supplier offering hundreds of different items, including air-drying clay, ceramic paint, and sketchbooks for kids.

Pearl River
477 Broadway
New York, NY 10013
212-431-4770
800-878-2446
www.pearlriver.com
Colorful, stylish, and affordable Chinese imports, including cute paper decorations, plain paper garlands, and a wide selection of origami papers.

Prizm
The Artist's Supply Store
5688 Mayfield Rd.
Cleveland, OH 44124
440-605-9434
Visit www.prizmart.comfor details of their other stores.
Paints, paper, clay and ceramics, markers and pens, and more art supplies.

Rag Shop
1616 N. Federal Hwy.
Boca Raton, FL 33432
561-750-1196
Visit www.ragshop.com for details of their other stores.
Art and crafts store with huge selection of paper, accessories, and more.

The Ribbonerie
191 Potrero Avenue
San Francisco, CA 94103
415-626-6184
www.theribbonerie.com
Extensive collection of gorgeous ribbons from around the world, including wired, grosgrain, metallic, velvet, and vintage examples.

Target
Locations nationwide
Visit www.target.com for details of your nearest store.
A good selection of varied crafting equipment is available from their children's toy departments. Craft kits, clay and pottery supplies, scrapbooking accessories, crafting tools, and more.

Tinsel Trading Co.
47 West 38th Street
New York, NY 10018
212-730-1030
www.tinseltrading.com
Vintage buttons and beads, as well as gorgeous silk and velvet flowers, sequins, metallic tassels, and ribbons.

The Ultimate Baker
1-866-285-COOK
www.cooksdream.com
Online cake-decorating supply store offering cookie cutters and rolling pins that are ideal for working with modeling clay.

Utrecht
Stores nationwide.
Visit www.utrechtart.com for details of your nearest store.
Useful source of discount art and craft supplies.

picture credits

ALL PHOTOGRAPHY BY VANESSA DAVIES

PAINT: pages 8–9 paints from Hobbycraft, paint dishes from Selwyn-Smith Studios, brushes from Sewing & Craft Superstore, Early Learning Centre; **pages 10–11** paints and plate from Brush & Bisque-It, striped aprons by Millie Mac; **pages 12–13** picture frame from Cargo Homeshop, plate from Brush & Bisque-It, tray from Mother Goose; **pages 14–15** potato printing paints from Hobbycraft, cookie cutter from Jane Asher Party Cakes; **pages 16–17** paper from Paperchase, calico fabric from John Lewis, picture frames and ribbon from IKEA; **pages 18–19** paints from Hobbycraft; **pages 20–21** paints from Hobbycraft; **pages 22–23** paints from Hobbycraft, fabric-covered notebooks from Paperchase; **pages 24–25** wooden lidded box from IKEA , heart and soldier stencils, brush, and stencil paint from The Stencil Library; **pages 26–27** calico and bias binding for aprons from John Lewis, stencils from The Stencil Library

FABRIC: pages 28–29 materials, satin ribbons, and wool from John Lewis, velvet ribbons and pipe cleaners from Paperchase, felt and pins from Sewing & Craft Superstore; **page 30–31** ribbons from Paperchase and John Lewis; **pages 32–33** colored pipe cleaners from Paperchase, ribbons from John Lewis and Paperchase; **pages 34–35** felt and three-dimensional fabric pens from Sewing & Craft Superstore; **pages 36–37** pompoms wool from John Lewis; **pages 38–39** wool from John Lewis, wool fabric from Sewing & Craft Superstore; **pages 40–41** lavender pockets felt, ribbon, and buttons from Sewing & Craft Superstore; **pages 42–43** collage felt, fabrics, and glue from Sewing & Craft Superstore, popsicle sticks from Hobbycraft; **pages 44–45** floral fabrics and spot china from Cath Kidston, tray (unpainted MDF) by Mother Goose, plain fabrics from Sewing & Craft Superstore, spot ribbon and trim on tea cozy from VV Rouleaux; **pages 46–47** dyes from Sewing & Craft Superstore

PAPER: pages 48–49 crêpe paper, pipe cleaners, and card all from Paperchase; **pages 50–53** crêpe paper, blank cards, and card all from Paperchase; **pages 54–55** paper from Paperchase, tassels from John Lewis, glitter and glue from Sewing & Craft Superstore, orange scissors from Early Learning Centre; **pages 56–57** colored paper from Sewing & Craft Superstore, wood from Hobbycraft; **pages 58–61** card from Sewing & Craft Superstore; **pages 62–63** paper from Paperchase; **pages 64–65** handmade papers and notebooks from Paperchase; **pages 66–67** boxes from Hobbycraft, handmade papers from Paperchase; **pages 68–69** paper from Paperchase, ribbon from Sewing & Craft Superstore; **pages 70–71** découpage handmade papers from Sewing & Craft Superstore, box from Muji; **pages 72–73** black-and-white playing-card paper from Dover Books, handmade papers from Paperchase, floral wallpaper from Laura Ashley, velvet ribbon from Sewing & Craft Superstore

MODELLING: pages 74–75 cookie cutters from Jane Asher Party Cakes, wooden spoons from Kooks Unlimited, wire from Hobbycraft; **pages 78–81** balsa wood, paints, popsicle sticks, and clothes-pegs from Hobbycraft, gingham from Sewing & Craft Superstore; **pages 82–83** jam jars from Kooks Unlimited, glitter from Hobbycraft, decorations from Homebase; **pages 84–85** clay and paints from Hobbycraft, cookie cutters from Jane Asher Party Cakes and Kooks Unlimited, paint dish from Selwyn-Smith

Studios; **pages 86–87** cookie cutters from Kooks Unlimited, butterfly, flower, and fish cookie cutters from Jane Asher Party Cakes, ribbon from VV Rouleaux, magnets and brooch backs from Sewing & Craft Superstore; **pages 88–89** wooden spoons from Kooks Unlimited, floral fabric from Cath Kidston, felt from Sewing & Craft Superstore, paper doilies from Jane Asher Party Cakes; **pages 90–91** wooden beads and wire from Sewing & Craft Superstore, plain colored beads and wire from Hobbycraft, glasses with beads from IKEA; **pages 92–93** balsa wood, paint, beads, modeling clay, and wire all from Hobbycraft

SPECIAL OCCASIONS: pages 94–95 clothes-peg dolls, sequins, and glitter from Hobbycraft, pompom, glitter, and sheer ribbon from Sewing & Craft Superstore, paint plate from Selwyn-Smith Studios, cupcake cups and doilies from Jane Asher Party Cakes; **pages 96–97** clothes-peg dolls from Hobbycraft, ribbon, lace, and silver card from Sewing & Craft Superstore; **pages 98–99** red and white paper from Hobbycraft; **pages 100–101** glitter card from Paperchase, sequins, pompoms, and silver pipe cleaner from Sewing & Craft Superstore, Christmas tree and lights from Woolworths; **pages 102–103** black card, silver paper, and black netting from Sewing & Craft Superstore, scissors from Early Learning Centre; **pages 104–105** black card, black felt, pompom, elastic, and pipe cleaners from Sewing & Craft Superstore, pencil and scissors from Early Learning Centre; **pages 106–107** doilies and cupcake cup from Jane Asher Party Cakes, sheer ribbon from Confetti; **pages 108–109** sheer ribbons and paintbrushes from Sewing & Craft Superstore, paints from Hobbycraft; **pages 110–111** paints and brushes from Hobbycraft; **pages 112–113** balsa and strip wood and paints from Hobbycraft, brushes and keyring chains from Sewing & Craft Superstore; **pages 114–115** cards and paper from Paperchase, ribbons, and decorative paper from Sewing & Craft Superstore; **pages 116–117** wooden picture frames from IKEA, handmade papers from Paperchase

index

acknowledgments Thank you to Vanessa Davies for her beautiful photography and attention to detail in the wonderful pictures she shot for the book. Thanks to Catherine Griffin and Annabel Morgan for their help at all stages of the book—its design, layout, and words. Thank you to all the fantastic children who modeled for the book—their patience during photography and their enthusiasm for the projects they worked on. Thanks also to Hobbycraft for supplying the wooden beads and The Stencil Library for the stencils. Finally, a big thank you to my husband Michael for his unfailing support and the delicious suppers he made when I had to work late to finish the projects for the book.